speedy

cooking in 20 minutes or less

THE AUSTRALIAN
Women's Weekly

CONTENTS

AUSTRALIAN CUP AND
SPOON MEASUREMENTS
ARE METRIC.
A CONVERSION CHART
APPEARS ON PAGE 77.

When you're in a hurry, the promise of dinner on the table in 20 minutes is too good to pass up. With only a few ingredients and a little imagination, speedy cooking is exciting, tasty and effortless.

Pamela Clark

Food Director

PRAWN, AVOCADO
AND MANGO SALAD

prep time 20 minutes **serves** 4
nutritional count per serving 8.9g total fat
(1.8g saturated fat); 1083kJ (259 cal);
19.7g carbohydrate; 23g protein; 3.3g fibre

2 small avocados (200g), chopped coarsely
2 tablespoons lime juice
2 medium mangoes (860g), chopped coarsely
800g (1½ pounds) cooked medium
    king prawns (shrimp)
80g (2½ ounces) mesclun

1 Blend or process avocado, juice and
2 tablespoons water until smooth. Place in
medium bowl.
2 Blend or process mango until smooth.
3 Shell and devein prawns, leaving tails intact.
4 Divide purees among serving plates; top with
mesclun and prawns.

SALADS

COUSCOUS SALAD WITH HALOUMI

prep + cook time **20 minutes** serves **4**
nutritional count per serving **45.4g total fat**
(16.4g saturated fat); 3641kJ (871 cal);
73g carbohydrate; 46.6g protein; 4.6g fibre

1½ cups (300g) couscous
1½ cups (375ml) boiling water
¼ cup (60ml) lemon juice
¼ cup (60ml) olive oil
1 teaspoon ground cumin
½ cup (70g) coarsely chopped dried dates
½ cup (70g) roasted slivered almonds
¾ cup coarsely chopped fresh mint
500g (1 pound) haloumi cheese, sliced thickly

1 Combine couscous with the water in
large heatproof bowl, cover; stand about
5 minutes or until liquid is absorbed, fluffing
with fork occasionally.
2 Combine juice, oil and cumin in screw-top
jar; shake well.
3 Add cumin dressing, dates, nuts and mint
to couscous; mix gently.
4 Heat oiled large frying pan; cook cheese
until browned both sides. Serve salad topped
with cheese.

warm balsamic and mushroom salad

WARM BALSAMIC
AND MUSHROOM SALAD

prep + cook time **10 minutes** serves **4**
nutritional count per serving **19.9g total fat**
(6g saturated fat); 1066kJ (255 cal);
3.1g carbohydrate; 14.6g protein; 3.8g fibre

8 slices pancetta (120g)
½ cup (125ml) balsamic italian dressing
500g (1 pound) small button mushrooms
1 teaspoon fresh thyme leaves
90g (3 ounces) mixed salad leaves
90g (3 ounces) fetta cheese, crumbled

1 Cook pancetta in heated oiled large frying
pan until crisp. When cool enough to handle,
break into large pieces.
2 Heat dressing and ⅓ cup (80ml) water in
same frying pan; cook mushrooms and thyme,
stirring, until mushrooms are tender and liquid
has almost evaporated.
3 Combine mushrooms, salad leaves and
pancetta in large bowl; toss gently. Serve
topped with cheese.

couscous salad with haloumi

chickpea and walnut salad with green chilli

CHICKPEA AND WALNUT SALAD WITH GREEN CHILLI

prep time **20 minutes** serves **8**
nutritional count per serving **17.7g total fat**
(1.8g saturated fat); 1053kJ (252 cal);
14.7g carbohydrate; 6.6g protein; 5.1g fibre

¼ cup (60ml) olive oil
¼ cup (60ml) lemon juice
800g (1½ pounds) canned chickpeas
   (garbanzos), rinsed, drained
1 cup coarsely chopped fresh
   flat-leaf parsley
1 cup coarsely chopped fresh mint
1 cup (160g) seeded green olives,
   chopped coarsely
4 green onions (scallions), sliced thinly
2 fresh long green chillies, sliced thinly
1 medium red capsicum (bell pepper)
   (200g), chopped finely
1 cup (100g) roasted walnuts,
   chopped coarsely

1 To make dressing, place oil and juice in
screw-top jar; shake well.
2 Combine remaining ingredients in large bowl;
drizzle with dressing before serving.

egg salad with croûtons

EGG SALAD WITH CROUTONS

prep time **15 minutes** serves **4**
nutritional count per serving **18.1g total fat**
(4.1g saturated fat); 1099kJ (263 cal);
13.2g carbohydrate; 10g protein; 4.2g fibre

1 medium butter (boston) lettuce,
   leaves separated
250g (8 ounces) cherry tomatoes, halved
2 shallots (50g), sliced thinly
⅓ cup (80ml) ranch dressing
4 hard-boiled eggs, halved
75g (2½ ounces) packaged croûtons

1 Divide lettuce, tomato, shallot and dressing
among serving bowls.
2 Serve topped with egg and croûtons.

smoked chicken and cranberry salad

ORANGE, BEETROOT AND ROAST BEEF SALAD

prep time 15 minutes serves 4
nutritional count per serving 19.9g total fat
(8.4g saturated fat); 1860kJ (445 cal);
26.8g carbohydrate; 36.4g protein; 6.2g fibre

2 medium oranges (480g)
400g (12½ ounces) shaved rare roast beef
850g (1¾ pounds) canned whole baby
    beetroot (beets), drained, halved
150g (4½ ounces) baby rocket
    (arugula) leaves
½ cup (125ml) buttermilk
¼ cup (75g) mayonnaise
1 tablespoon wholegrain mustard
100g (3 ounces) blue cheese, crumbled

1 Segment oranges over large bowl; reserve 1 tablespoon juice separately.
2 Add beef, beetroot and rocket to bowl.
3 Whisk reserved juice with buttermilk, mayonnaise and mustard in small bowl. Sprinkle cheese over salad; drizzle with dressing.

SMOKED CHICKEN AND CRANBERRY SALAD

prep time 15 minutes serves 4
nutritional count per serving 39.8g total fat
(5.2g saturated fat); 2420kJ (579 cal);
17.7g carbohydrate; 35.5g protein; 5.9g fibre

2 teaspoons dijon mustard
¼ cup (60ml) apple cider vinegar
2 tablespoons olive oil
500g (1 pound) smoked chicken breast
    fillets, sliced thinly
1 large green apple (200g), sliced thinly
1 cup (120g) roasted pecans
½ cup (65g) craisins
150g (4½ ounces) baby spinach leaves
1 cup loosely packed fresh parsley leaves

1 Place mustard, vinegar and oil in screw-top jar; shake well.
2 Combine dressing with remaining ingredients in large bowl.

orange, beetroot and roast beef salad

WITLOF, PEAR AND BLUE CHEESE SALAD

prep time **20 minutes** serves **4**
nutritional count per serving **24.9g total fat**
(6.5g saturated fat); 1295kJ (309 cal);
9.9g carbohydrate; 9.5g protein; 5.3g fibre

2 red witlof (belgian endive) (250g), trimmed,
  leaves separated
2 yellow witlof (belgian endive) (250g),
  trimmed, leaves separated
1 medium pear (230g), sliced thinly
¾ cup (90g) roasted pecans,
  coarsely chopped
blue cheese dressing
⅓ cup (80ml) buttermilk
100g (3 ounces) blue cheese, crumbled
1 tablespoon lemon juice

1 Make blue cheese dressing.
2 Combine salad ingredients in large bowl.
3 Serve salad drizzled with blue cheese dressing.
blue cheese dressing Whisk ingredients in
small jug until smooth.

tip Witlof, or belgian endive, or chicory has a tightly
bunched, elongated head. To minimise bitterness it is
grown in the dark.

waldorf salad

WARM PORK AND MANDARIN SALAD WITH HONEY DRESSING

prep + cook time 20 minutes serves 4
nutritional count per serving 27.2g total fat
(5g saturated fat); 2098kJ (502 cal);
20.7g carbohydrate; 41g protein; 5.9g fibre

600g (1¼ pounds) pork fillets
2 medium mandarins (400g), peeled
2 tablespoons olive oil
1 tablespoon honey
1 fresh long red chilli, chopped finely
2 medium radicchio (400g), trimmed
1 cup (50g) snow pea sprouts
¾ cup (115g) roasted unsalted cashews

1 Cook pork, uncovered, in heated oiled large frying pan until cooked as desired. Cover; stand 5 minutes then slice thickly.
2 Meanwhile, segment mandarins into large bowl. Add oil, honey and chilli; stir gently to combine. Add pork, radicchio, sprouts and nuts; toss salad, serve warm.

WALDORF SALAD

prep time 20 minutes serves 4
nutritional count per serving 35.7g total fat
(3.1g saturated fat); 1852kJ (443 cal);
22.4g carbohydrate; 5.8g protein; 6.3g fibre

¾ cup (225g) mayonnaise
¼ cup (60ml) lemon juice
5 celery stalks (750g), trimmed, sliced thickly
2 medium red apples (300g), sliced thinly
1 small red onion (100g), sliced thinly
1 cup (100g) roasted walnuts
1 cup loosely packed fresh flat-leaf
    parsley leaves

1 Combine mayonnaise and juice in large bowl; mix in remaining ingredients.

warm pork and mandarin salad with honey dressing

fattoush

FATTOUSH

prep + cook time **20 minutes** serves **4**
nutritional count per serving **19.7g total fat**
(2.7g saturated fat); 1367kJ (327 cal);
28.1g carbohydrate; 6.8g protein; 5.8g fibre

2 large pitta bread (160g)
⅓ cup (80ml) olive oil
2 tablespoons lemon juice
1 clove garlic, crushed
3 red radishes (100g), trimmed, sliced thinly
½ small daikon (200g), grated coarsely
2 medium tomatoes (300g),
    chopped coarsely
1 lebanese cucumber (130g),
    chopped coarsely
1 small red onion (100g), sliced thinly
1 small green capsicum (bell pepper) (150g),
    chopped coarsely
1 cup loosely packed fresh mint leaves
1 cup loosely packed fresh flat-leaf
    parsley leaves

1 Preheat grill (broiler) to hot.
2 Place bread on oven tray; grill until crisp.
Break bread into pieces.
3 Whisk oil, juice and garlic together in
large bowl. Mix in half the bread crisps and
remaining ingredients.
4 Serve fattoush sprinkled with remaining
bread crisps.

mexican beef salad

MEXICAN BEEF SALAD

prep + cook time **15 minutes** serves **4**
nutritional count per serving **10.7g total fat**
(4.6g saturated fat); 1392kJ (333 cal);
15.9g carbohydrate; 39.8g protein; 6.6g fibre

35g (1 ounce) packaged taco seasoning mix
600g (1¼-pound) piece beef rump steak
420g (13½ ounces) canned four-bean mix,
    rinsed, drained
125g (4 ounces) canned corn kernels,
    rinsed, drained
2 large tomatoes (440g), chopped finely
½ cup coarsely chopped fresh
    coriander (cilantro)

1 Rub seasoning mix over both sides of beef.
Cook beef in heated oiled large frying pan.
Remove from pan; cover, stand 5 minutes then
slice thickly.
2 Meanwhile, combine beans, corn, tomato
and coriander in medium bowl; season to
taste. Divide salad between serving plates; top
with beef. Serve with lime wedges, if you like.

RUBY GRAPEFRUIT, POMEGRANATE AND ENDIVE SALAD

prep time **15 minutes**   serves **4**
nutritional count per serving **23.7g total fat**
(2.5g saturated fat); 1208kJ (289 cal);
12.8g carbohydrate; 4.5g protein; 4.6g fibre

3 ruby red grapefruit (1kg)
¼ cup (60ml) olive oil
2 tablespoons coarsely chopped
  fresh chervil
100g (3 ounces) curly endive leaves
½ cup pomegranate pulp
½ cup (55g) coarsely chopped
  roasted walnuts

1 Juice half of one grapefruit; reserve juice.
Peel remaining grapefruit; slice thickly.
2 To make dressing, place reserved juice, oil
and chervil in screw-top jar; shake well.
3 Toss endive and dressing in large bowl.
Layer endive, grapefruit and pomegranate on
serving plate; serve sprinkled with nuts.

tip You need 1 medium pomegranate for this recipe.
Pomegranate pulp consists of the seeds and the edible
pulp surrounding them; it has a tangy sweet-sour
flavour. To remove the seeds, cut the fruit in half
crossways and hold each half cut-side down over a
bowl. Hit the outside skin of the fruit sharply with a
wooden spoon – as hard as you can – the seeds should
fall out – if they don't, dig them out with a teaspoon.

MINI CABANOSSI PIZZA

prep + cook time **20 minutes** makes **12**
nutritional count per pizza **5.1g total fat
(2.1g saturated fat); 644kJ (154 cal);
19.6g carbohydrate; 6.5g protein; 1.5g fibre**

Preheat oven to 220°C/425°F. Line oven tray
with baking paper. Cut 12 x 6.5cm (2½-inch)
fluted rounds from a 440g (14-ounce) pizza
base with sauce; place on tray. Top pizza
rounds with 1 coarsely grated medium
zucchini, 100g (3 ounces) thinly sliced
cabanossi and 12 torn cherry bocconcini
cheeses. Bake about 5 minutes or until
heated through.

PANINI WITH CHORIZO

prep + cook time **20 minutes** makes **8**
nutritional count per serving **39.9g total fat
(12.6g saturated fat); 3018kJ (722 cal);
60.2g carbohydrate; 28.9g protein; 4.1g fibre**

Cook 3 thickly sliced smoked chorizo sausages
in heated oiled large frying pan, in batches,
until browned. Drain on absorbent paper.
Combine 1 cup (300g) mayonnaise and
½ teaspoon smoked paprika in small bowl.
Split 8 panini rolls in half; spread mayonnaise
mixture over roll halves.
Top with chorizo, 5 thinly sliced hard-boiled
eggs, 80g (2½ ounces) baby spinach leaves,
150g (4½ ounces) shaved manchego cheese
and remaining panini half.
tip Manchego cheese is Spanish; it is available from
specialist cheese stores and Spanish delicatessens.
If you can't find it, use parmesan cheese instead. Use a
vegetable peeler to shave the cheese.

SPEEDY SNACKS

BEAN NACHOS

prep + cook time **20 minutes** serves **6**
nutritional count per serving **24.5g total fat**
(11.6g saturated fat); 1856kJ (444 cal);
33.7g carbohydrate; 17.3g protein; 10.8g fibre

Preheat oven to 220°C/425°F. Combine 420g
(13½ ounces) canned, rinsed, drained kidney
beans with ⅓ cup chunky tomato salsa in a
medium bowl; mash until chunky. Stir in 420g
(13½ ounces) canned, rinsed, drained kidney
beans and ⅓ cup finely chopped fresh
coriander (cilantro). Spread 115g (3½ ounces)
corn chips in medium shallow baking dish; top
with ¾ cup (90g) coarsely grated cheddar
cheese and half the bean mixture. Top with
115g (3½ ounces) extra corn chips, ¾ cup
(90g) extra coarsely grated cheddar cheese
then remaining bean mixture. Cook 10 minutes.
Toss 2 cups finely shredded lettuce, 1 coarsely
chopped small tomato and ½ coarsely
chopped small avocado in medium bowl with
2 tablespoons lime juice. Serve with salad.

VIETNAMESE PRAWN ROLLS

prep time **20 minutes** makes **12**
nutritional count per roll **0.9g total fat**
(0.1g saturated fat); 326kJ (78 cal);
10.8g carbohydrate; 5.5g protein; 1.7g fibre

Combine 50g soaked, drained rice vermicelli
noodles in medium bowl with ¼ finely shredded
small wombok (napa cabbage), ½ cup loosely
packed torn fresh mint leaves, 2 teaspoons
light brown sugar and 2 tablespoons lime juice.
Shell and devein 500g (1 pound) cooked
medium king prawns (shrimp); chop prawns
finely. Combine ½ cup (125ml) hoisin sauce
and 2 tablespoons rice vinegar in a small bowl.
Dip a 21cm (8½-inch) rice paper round into
bowl of warm water until soft; place on board
covered with tea towel. Top with a little of the
prawn meat and noodle filling. Fold and roll to
enclose filling. Repeat to make 12 rice paper
rolls. Serve with hoisin dipping sauce.

PEKING DUCK IN A WOK

prep + cook time 20 minutes serves 4
nutritional count per serving 40.6g total fat
(11.6g saturated fat); 2713kJ (649 cal);
35.1g carbohydrate; 33.5g protein; 7.3g fibre

1 chinese barbecued duck (1kg)
24 peking duck pancakes (240g)
4 green onions (scallions), cut into thin strips
⅔ cup (160ml) hoisin sauce
2 cups (160g) bean sprouts
2 lebanese cucumbers (260g), halved
    lengthways, seeded, cut into thin strips

1 Remove meat and skin from duck; discard
bones. Chop meat and skin coarsely.
2 Meanwhile, heat pancakes by folding each
into quarters, place in steamer set over large
pan of simmering water; steam until warm
and pliable.
3 Heat wok; stir-fry duck and onion until
onion just softens. Add half the sauce;
stir-fry until hot.
4 Remove from heat; stir in sprouts. Serve
duck mixture with pancakes, cucumber and
remaining sauce.
tip Buy a barbecued duck and a packet of peking duck
pancakes at an Asian food shop on your way home from
work and you'll have a great dinner on the table in a few
minutes – so easy and so delicious.

STIR-FRIES

fried rice with tomato, pineapple and snow peas

1 Heat oil in wok; stir-fry snow peas, onion and garlic until snow peas are tender. Add rice, sauces and juice; stir-fry until hot.
2 Remove from heat; stir in pineapple and tomato, season to taste.

tip You need to cook about 1⅓ cups (265g) white long-grain rice the day before making this recipe. Spread it evenly onto a tray and refrigerate overnight.

SWEET AND SOY PORK

prep + cook time 20 minutes serves 4
nutritional count per serving 12g total fat
(2.7g saturated fat); 1622kJ (388 cal);
34.6g carbohydrate; 34g protein; 2.2g fibre

500g (1 pound) fresh wide rice noodles
1½ tablespoons peanut oil
500g (1 pound) pork fillet, sliced thinly
300g (9½ ounces) gai lan, chopped coarsely
3 cloves garlic, crushed
2 tablespoons light soy sauce
2 tablespoons dark soy sauce
2 tablespoons light brown sugar
1 egg

1 Place noodles in large heatproof bowl, cover with boiling water; separate with fork, drain.
2 Heat 1 tablespoon of the oil in wok; stir-fry pork, in batches, until browned. Remove from wok.
3 Separate leaves and stems from gai lan. Heat remaining oil in wok; stir-fry gai lan stems until tender. Add gai lan leaves and garlic; stir-fry until gai lan wilts. Return pork to wok with noodles, sauces and sugar; stir-fry until hot.
4 Make a well in centre of noodles, add egg; stir-fry egg until egg and noodle mixture are combined.

FRIED RICE WITH TOMATO, PINEAPPLE AND SNOW PEAS

prep + cook time 20 minutes serves 4
nutritional count per serving 5.4g total fat
(0.8g saturated fat); 1354kJ (324 cal);
57.1g carbohydrate; 8.4g protein; 4.7g fibre

1 tablespoon peanut oil
200g (6½ ounces) snow peas, trimmed, sliced thickly
4 green onions (scallions), sliced thinly
2 cloves garlic, crushed
4 cups cooked white long-grain rice
¼ cup (60ml) japanese soy sauce
1 tablespoon fish sauce
1 tablespoon lime juice
500g (1 pound) pineapple, peeled, cored, cut into 1cm (½-inch) pieces
2 medium tomatoes (300g), seeded, cut into 1cm (½-inch) pieces

sweet and soy pork

fish with kaffir lime and sugar snap peas

FISH WITH KAFFIR LIME AND SUGAR SNAP PEAS

prep + cook time **20 minutes** serves **4**
nutritional count per serving **12.1g total fat**
(2.5g saturated fat); 1158kJ (277 cal); 11.2g
carbohydrate; 29.5g protein; 3g fibre

2 tablespoons peanut oil
500g (1 pound) firm white fish fillets, cut into
   3cm (1¼-inch) pieces
1 medium brown onion (150g), sliced thinly
1 clove garlic, crushed
10cm (4-inch) stick fresh lemon grass (20g),
   chopped finely
1½ tablespoons light brown sugar
½ cup (125ml) water
300g (9½ ounces) sugar snap peas, trimmed
170g (5½ ounces) asparagus, trimmed, cut
   into 3cm (1¼-inch) lengths
2 kaffir lime leaves, shredded finely
2 tablespoons lemon juice

1 Heat half the oil in wok; stir-fry fish, in
batches, until browned. Remove from wok.
2 Heat remaining oil in wok; stir-fry onion,
garlic and lemon grass until onion softens. Add
sugar and half the water; bring to the boil.
Simmer, uncovered, until sauce thickens slightly.
3 Add peas, asparagus and the remaining
water; stir-fry until vegetables are tender.
Return fish to wok; stir-fry until hot.
4 Serve stir-fry sprinkled with lime leaves;
drizzle with lemon juice.

honeyed ginger chicken

HONEYED GINGER CHICKEN

prep + cook time **20 minutes** serves **4**
nutritional count per serving **15.5g total fat**
(3.5g saturated fat); 1292kJ (309 cal);
15.6g carbohydrate; 26.4g protein; 2.1g fibre

500g (1 pound) chicken thigh fillets,
   chopped coarsely
4cm (1½-inch) piece fresh ginger (20g), grated
1 teaspoon five-spice powder
2 tablespoons peanut oil
170g (5½ ounces) asparagus, trimmed,
   cut into 3cm (1¼-inch) lengths
2 tablespoons dark soy sauce
2 tablespoons honey
1 tablespoon water
250g (8 ounces) snow peas, trimmed, halved

1 Combine chicken, ginger, five-spice and half
the oil in medium bowl.
2 Heat half the remaining oil in wok; stir-fry
chicken, in batches, until browned. Remove
from wok.
3 Heat remaining oil in wok; stir-fry asparagus
until tender. Return chicken to wok with sauce,
honey, the water and peas; stir-fry until hot.

EGG NOODLES WITH CHICKEN

prep + cook time **20 minutes** serves **4**
nutritional count per serving **16.3g total fat**
(3.6g saturated fat); 1701kJ (407 cal);
30.4g carbohydrate; 30.9g protein; 4g fibre

500g (1 pound) chicken thigh fillets,
   sliced thinly
2 tablespoons tamari
2 tablespoons mirin
4cm (1½-inch) piece fresh ginger (20g), grated
2 cloves garlic, crushed
440g (14 ounces) thin egg noodles
2 tablespoons peanut oil
8 green onions (scallions), cut into 4cm
   (1½-inch) lengths
500g (1 pound) baby buk choy,
   chopped coarsely

1 Combine chicken, tamari, mirin, ginger and garlic in medium bowl.
2 Place noodles in large heatproof bowl, cover with boiling water; separate with fork, drain.
3 Drain chicken, reserve marinade. Heat half the oil in wok; stir-fry chicken, in batches, until browned. Remove from wok.
4 Heat remaining oil in same cleaned wok; stir-fry onion until softened. Return chicken to wok with reserved marinade; bring to the boil. Add noodles and buk choy; stir-fry until buk choy wilts.

tip Chicken mixture can be marinated for 30 minutes or overnight.

LAMB WITH SPINACH AND RICE NOODLES

prep + cook time **20 minutes** serves **4**
nutritional count per serving **12.5g total fat**
(3.9g saturated fat); 1396kJ (334 cal);
15.2g carbohydrate; 38.4g protein; 1.7g fibre

300g (9½ ounces) dried rice noodles
500g (1 pound) lamb fillets, sliced thinly
300g (9½ ounces) spinach, trimmed,
   shredded coarsely
2 cloves garlic, crushed
¼ cup (60ml) kecap manis
1 tablespoon japanese soy sauce

1 Place noodles in large heatproof bowl, cover with boiling water; stand until tender, drain.
2 Heat oiled wok; stir-fry lamb, in batches, until browned, remove lamb from wok.
3 Reheat wok; stir-fry spinach and garlic until spinach wilts. Return lamb to wok with noodles and sauces; stir-fry until hot.

udon with chilli and mixed vegetables

UDON WITH CHILLI AND MIXED VEGETABLES

prep + cook time **20 minutes** serves **4**
nutritional count per serving **8.1g total fat**
(1.1g saturated fat); 1083kJ (259 cal);
37.4g carbohydrate; 6.5g protein; 4.7g fibre

440g (14 ounces) fresh udon noodles
400g (12½ ounces) packaged traditional
   stir-fry vegetables
100g (3 ounces) enoki mushrooms
2 fresh long red chillies, sliced thinly
¼ cup (75g) harissa paste

1 Place noodles in large heatproof bowl, cover with boiling water; separate with fork, drain.
2 Heat oiled wok; stir-fry vegetables, mushrooms and chilli until vegetables are tender. Add noodles and paste; stir-fry until hot.
tip **Add harissa to taste as different brands vary in heat.**

spiced pumpkin and chickpeas

STIR-FRIED PORK WITH BUK CHOY AND RICE NOODLES

prep + cook time **20 minutes** serves **4**
nutritional count per serving **6.7g total fat**
(1.6g saturated fat); 1492kJ (357 cal);
31.6g carbohydrate; 37.9g protein; 2.9g fibre

¼ cup (60ml) oyster sauce
2 tablespoons light soy sauce
2 tablespoons sweet sherry
1 tablespoon light brown sugar
1 clove garlic, crushed
1 star anise, crushed
pinch five-spice powder
400g (12½ ounces) fresh rice noodles
2 teaspoons sesame oil
600g (1¼ pounds) pork fillets, sliced thinly
700g (1½ pounds) baby buk choy,
    chopped coarsely

1 Combine sauces, sherry, sugar, garlic, star anise and five-spice in small jug.
2 Place noodles in large heatproof bowl, cover with boiling water; separate with fork, drain.
3 Heat oil in wok; stir-fry pork, in batches, until cooked as desired. Return pork to wok with sauce mixture, noodles and buk choy; stir-fry until buk choy is wilted.

SPICED PUMPKIN AND CHICKPEAS

prep + cook time **20 minutes** serves **4**
nutritional count per serving **11g total fat**
(2.1g saturated fat); 828kJ (198 cal);
15.5g carbohydrate; 7.2g protein; 5.4g fibre

2 tablespoons peanut oil
500g (1 pound) pumpkin, cut into
    1cm (½-inch) pieces
1 tablespoon chermoula spice mix
420g (13½ ounces) canned chickpeas
    (garbanzos), rinsed, drained
300g (9½ ounces) spinach, trimmed,
    chopped coarsely

1 Heat oil in wok; stir-fry pumpkin about 6 minutes or until almost tender.
2 Add spice mix; stir-fry about 2 minutes or until pumpkin is tender.
3 Add chickpeas and spinach; stir-fry until spinach wilts.

stir-fried pork with buk choy and rice noodles

BEEF KWAY TEO

prep + cook time **20 minutes** serves **4**
nutritional count per serving **21.8g total fat**
(6.8g saturated fat); 2362kJ (565 cal);
54.2g carbohydrate; 33.7g protein; 3.6g fibre

¼ cup (60ml) oyster sauce
2 tablespoons kecap manis
2 tablespoons chinese cooking wine
1 teaspoon sambal oelek
3 cloves garlic, crushed
2cm (¾-inch) piece fresh ginger (10g), grated
2 tablespoons peanut oil
500g (1 pound) beef strips
450g (14½ ounces) fresh wide rice noodles
6 green onions (scallions), cut into
    2cm (¾-inch) lengths
1 medium red capsicum (bell pepper)
    (200g), sliced thinly
¼ cup (15g) coarsely chopped garlic chives
2 cups (160g) bean sprouts

1 Combine sauces, cooking wine, sambal,
garlic and ginger in small jug.
2 Heat half the oil in wok; stir-fry beef, in
batches, until browned.
3 Meanwhile, place noodles in large heatproof
bowl, cover with boiling water; separate with
fork, drain.
4 Heat remaining oil in wok; stir-fry onion and
capsicum until capsicum is tender.
5 Return beef to wok with sauce mixture,
noodles, chives and sprouts; stir-fry until hot.

tip Garlic chives have rougher, flatter leaves than simple
chives, and possess a pink-tinged teardrop-shaped
flowering bud at the end. They can be used as
a salad green, or steamed and eaten as a vegetable.

teriyaki beef and soba stir-fry

SINGAPORE NOODLES

prep + cook time **20 minutes** serves **4**
nutritional count per serving **15.5g total fat**
(4.6g saturated fat); 1944kJ (465 cal);
32.7g carbohydrate; 41.9g protein; 3.2g fibre

450g (14½ ounces) fresh singapore noodles
1 teaspoon peanut oil
1 small brown onion (80g), sliced finely
2 rindless bacon slices (130g),
    chopped finely
3cm (1¼-inch) piece fresh ginger (15g), grated
1 tablespoon mild curry powder
3 cups (480g) shredded barbecued chicken
6 green onions (scallions), sliced thinly
1½ tablespoons light soy sauce
⅓ cup (80ml) sweet sherry

1 Place noodles in large heatproof bowl, cover
with boiling water; separate with fork, drain.
2 Heat oil in wok; stir-fry brown onion, bacon
and ginger, about 2 minutes or until onion
softens and bacon is crisp. Add curry powder;
stir-fry until fragrant.
3 Add noodles and remaining ingredients;
stir-fry until hot.
tip You need to buy a large barbecued chicken to get
the amount of shredded meat needed for this recipe.

TERIYAKI BEEF
AND SOBA STIR-FRY

prep + cook time **20 minutes** serves **4**
nutritional count per serving **18.9g total fat**
(5.5g saturated fat); 2245kJ (537 cal);
47.8g carbohydrate; 41.5g protein; 3.8g fibre

270g (8½ ounces) dried soba noodles
2 tablespoons peanut oil
600g (1¼ pounds) beef eye fillet, sliced thinly
6 green onions (scallions), cut into
    5cm (2-inch) lengths
⅓ cup (80ml) teriyaki sauce
2 cups (160g) bean sprouts

1 Cook noodles in large saucepan of boiling
water, uncovered, until tender; drain.
2 Meanwhile, heat oil in wok; stir-fry beef until
browned. Add onion to wok; stir-fry until soft.
Add sauce and noodles to wok; stir-fry until
heated through. Remove from heat; add
sprouts to wok, toss to combine.

singapore noodles

BRUSCHETTA WITH TOMATO, BASIL AND CAPERS

prep + cook time **15 minutes** serves **6**
nutritional count per serving **8.4g total fat**
(1.2g saturated fat); 1183kJ (283 cal);
40.6g carbohydrate; 8.5g protein; 4.3g fibre

Seed and finely dice 6 ripe tomatoes; combine
in medium bowl with 2 tablespoons extra virgin
olive oil, ¼ cup fresh baby basil leaves and
2 tablespoons rinsed, drained baby capers.
Cut 500g (1 pound) loaf wood-fired bread into
12 slices; toast slices both sides on heated
oiled grill plate (or grill or barbecue). Rub one
side of each slice with the cut side of a garlic
clove; place toast on platter, garlic-side up.
Top toasts with tomato mixture; sprinkle with
freshly ground black pepper and drizzle with
extra olive oil.

OYSTERS WITH MIRIN AND CUCUMBER

prep + cook time **10 minutes** serves **6**
nutritional count per serving **11.6g total fat**
(4.3g saturated fat); 1526kJ (365 cal);
4g carbohydrate; 59g protein; 0.3g fibre

Whisk 2 tablespoons mirin, 1 tablespoon
salt-reduced soy sauce and 1 tablespoon lime
juice in small bowl. Peel 1 lebanese cucumber
randomly, halve lengthways; remove seeds,
dice finely. Slice 3 green onions (scallions)
diagonally. Place 48 oysters on the half shell
on serving platter or plates. Drizzle mirin
dressing over oysters; sprinkle with cucumber,
onion and freshly ground black pepper.

SPEEDY STARTERS

OREGANO BAKED FETTA

prep + cook time **15 minutes** serves **6**
nutritional count per serving **10.8g total fat**
(5.5g saturated fat); 502kJ (120 cal);
0.1g carbohydrate; 5.9g protein; 0g fibre

Preheat oven to 200°C/400°F. Place 200g
(6½-ounce) piece fetta cheese in small
ovenproof dish; sprinkle with 1 tablespoon
extra virgin olive oil, 1 tablespoon coarsely
chopped fresh oregano leaves, ¼ teaspoon
sweet paprika and freshly ground black pepper.
Bake, covered, about 10 minutes or until
cheese is heated through. Serve fetta warm
from dish, with a sliced french bread loaf and
seeded black olives.

CROSTINI WITH GOAT'S CHEESE, ARTICHOKES AND ROCKET

prep + cook time **20 minutes** serves **6**
nutritional count per serving **5.8g total fat**
(2.8g saturated fat); 535kJ (128 cal);
11.9g carbohydrate; 6g protein; 2g fibre

Preheat oven to 180°C/350°F. To make
crostini, slice 1 small french bread stick into
8mm (½-inch)-thick rounds. Spray both sides
with olive-oil spray; toast on oven tray. Rub
one side of each crostini with cut side of garlic
clove; place crostini on platter. Combine 30g
(1 ounce) baby rocket (arugula) leaves with
1 teaspoon each of extra virgin olive oil and
red wine vinegar in medium bowl. Cut 5
drained marinated artichoke hearts into
6 wedges each. Top crostini with rocket
mixture, then artichokes; sprinkle with 100g
(3 ounces) coarsely crumbled fetta cheese and
freshly ground black pepper.

PRAWN AND PESTO LINGUINE

prep + cook time 10 minutes **serves** 4
nutritional count per serving 19.8g total fat
(4.2g saturated fat); 2571kJ (615 cal);
65.1g carbohydrate; 40.9g protein; 4.9g fibre

375g (12 ounces) linguine pasta
500g (1 pound) shelled uncooked large
    green prawns (shrimp)
2 cloves garlic, crushed
1 fresh long red chilli, sliced thinly
1 medium zucchini (120g), cut into ribbons
180g (6 ounces) bottled chunky basil
    pesto dip

1 Cook pasta in large saucepan of boiling
water until tender; drain, reserving ⅓ cup
(80ml) cooking liquid. Return pasta to pan.
2 Meanwhile, heat oiled large frying pan;
cook prawns until changed in colour. Add
garlic, chilli and zucchini to pan; cook,
uncovered, until zucchini softens.
3 Add pesto, prawn mixture and reserved
cooking liquid to pasta; toss gently.
tip Use a vegetable peeler to cut the zucchini
into ribbons.

SPICY CHICKEN TACOS

prep + cook time 20 minutes makes 10
nutritional count per taco 35.9g total fat
(13.3g saturated fat); 2445kJ (585 cal);
29.7g carbohydrate; 33.2g protein; 6.7g fibre

1 tablespoon olive oil
1 medium brown onion (150g),
    chopped finely
500g (1 pound) minced (ground) chicken
35g (1 ounce) packaged taco seasoning mix
375g (12 ounces) bottled
    thick and chunky taco sauce
½ cup (125ml) water
10 stand'n'stuff taco shells (140g)
1 cup finely shredded iceberg lettuce
1 medium carrot (120g), coarsely grated
125g (4 ounces) cherry tomatoes, quartered
½ cup (60g) coarsely grated cheddar cheese
½ cup loosely packed fresh coriander
    (cilantro) leaves
⅓ cup (80g) sour cream

1 Heat oil in large frying pan, add onion; cook, stirring, until softened. Add chicken; cook, stirring, until browned. Add taco seasoning, cook, stirring, until fragrant. Add half the taco sauce and the water; cook, stirring occasionally, about 5 minutes or until mixture thickens. Remove from heat.

2 Meanwhile, heat taco shells according to directions on packet.

3 Divide chicken mixture into shells; top with lettuce, carrot, tomato, cheese, coriander and remaining sauce. Serve topped with sour cream.

peppered steaks with creamy bourbon sauce

PEPPERED STEAKS WITH CREAMY BOURBON SAUCE

prep + cook time **20 minutes** serves **4**
nutritional count per serving **49.3g total fat**
(25.9g saturated fat); 2742kJ (656 cal);
13.2g carbohydrate; 28.7g protein; 0.7g fibre

4 x 125g (4-ounce) beef fillet steaks
2 teaspoons cracked black pepper
2 tablespoons olive oil
6 shallots (150g), sliced thinly
1 clove garlic, crushed
⅓ cup (80ml) bourbon
¼ cup (60ml) beef stock
2 teaspoons dijon mustard
1¼ cups (310ml) pouring cream

1 Rub beef all over with pepper. Heat half the
oil in large frying pan; cook beef, uncovered,
until cooked as desired. Remove from pan;
cover to keep warm.
2 Heat remaining oil in same pan; cook shallot
and garlic, stirring, until shallot softens. Add
bourbon; stir until mixture simmers and starts
to thicken. Add remaining ingredients; bring to
the boil. Reduce heat; simmer, uncovered,
about 5 minutes or until sauce thickens slightly.
3 Serve beef drizzled with sauce.

tip **It is fine to use just 1 x 300ml carton of cream for
this recipe.**

garlicky lemon chicken

GARLICKY LEMON CHICKEN

prep + cook time **10 minutes** serves **4**
nutritional count per serving **21.7g total fat**
(6.6g saturated fat); 1760kJ (421 cal);
0.6g carbohydrate; 56.1g protein; 0.6g fibre

6 chicken thigh fillets (660g), halved
2 tablespoons coarsely chopped fresh
**   flat-leaf parsley**
3 cloves garlic, crushed
2 teaspoons finely grated lemon rind
2 tablespoons lemon juice
1 tablespoon water

1 Cook chicken in heated oiled large frying pan
until cooked through.
2 Add parsley, garlic, rind, juice and the water
to pan.
3 Turn chicken to coat in sauce; season with
black pepper, if you like.

RIGATONI WITH ZUCCHINI, LEMON AND MINT

prep + cook time **20 minutes** serves **4**
nutritional count per serving **30.3g total fat**
(6g saturated fat); 3110kJ (744 cal);
8.9g carbohydrate; 23.9g protein; 8.3g fibre

500g (1 pound) rigatoni pasta
¼ cup (60ml) olive oil
2 cloves garlic, crushed
3 medium zucchini (360g), grated coarsely
¾ cup (180g) ricotta cheese
1 cup coarsely chopped fresh mint
½ cup (70g) roasted slivered almonds
2 tablespoons lemon juice

1 Cook pasta in large saucepan of boiling water until just tender; drain.
2 Meanwhile, heat oil in large frying pan; cook garlic and zucchini, stirring, 2 minutes. Add cheese; cook, stirring, until just heated through.
3 Combine zucchini mixture and pasta in serving bowl with remaining ingredients.

pan-fried fish with fennel salad

PAN-FRIED FISH WITH FENNEL SALAD

prep + cook time **20 minutes** serves **4**
nutritional count per serving **13.9g total fat**
(2.7g saturated fat); 1409kJ (337 cal);
8.6g carbohydrate; 42.9g protein; 2.8g fibre

4 x 200g (6½-ounce) firm white fish
  fillets, skin-on
2 medium red capsicums (bell peppers)
  (400g), chopped coarsely
2 small fennel (400g), trimmed, sliced thinly
½ cup (60g) seeded black olives
⅓ cup coarsely chopped fresh basil
2 tablespoons olive oil
1 tablespoon balsamic vinegar

1 Cook fish, skin-side down, in heated oiled large frying pan, turning once, until cooked.
2 Meanwhile, combine remaining ingredients in medium bowl. Serve fish with salad.

rigatoni with zucchini, lemon and mint

spicy squid and tomato linguine

SPICY SQUID AND TOMATO LINGUINE

prep + cook time **25 minutes** serves **4**
nutritional count per serving **3g total fat**
(0.7g saturated fat); 1919kJ (459 cal);
70.5g carbohydrate; 33.3g protein; 5.9g fibre

375g (12 ounces) linguine pasta
2 cloves garlic, crushed
1 teaspoon dried chilli flakes
800g (28 ounces) canned crushed tomatoes
500g (1 pound) cleaned squid hoods,
**   sliced thinly**
30g (1 ounce) baby rocket leaves (arugula)

1 Cook pasta in large saucepan of boiling water until tender; drain.
2 Meanwhile, cook garlic and chilli flakes in heated oiled large frying pan, stirring, until fragrant. Add undrained tomatoes; bring to the boil. Reduce heat; simmer, uncovered, about 10 minutes or until sauce thickens slightly.
3 Add squid to tomato sauce; cook, stirring occasionally, about 5 minutes or until squid is tender. Season to taste.
4 Combine hot pasta and sauce; serve with rocket.

spicy fish burgers

SPICY FISH BURGERS

prep + cook time **20 minutes** serves **4**
nutritional count per serving **15.2g total fat**
(2.5g saturated fat); 1726kJ (413 cal);
26.5g carbohydrate; 40.9g protein; 2.7g fibre

4 x 180g (5½-ounce) firm white fish fillets
2 tablespoons piri piri spice mix
4 crusty bread rolls, split
½ cup (150g) mayonnaise
2 tablespoons finely chopped fresh dill
1 baby cos lettuce (180g), trimmed,
**   leaves separated**

1 Sprinkle fish with spice mix.
2 Cook fish in heated oiled large frying pan. Meanwhile, preheat grill (broiler) and toast cut sides of rolls until golden. Spread with combined mayonnaise and dill.
3 Sandwich rolls with lettuce leaves and fish.

beef rissoles with beetroot salad

SMOKY BEANS WITH CHORIZO

prep + cook time **10 minutes** serves **6**
nutritional count per serving **9.4g total fat**
(3.3g saturated fat); 1225kJ (293 cal);
33g carbohydrate; 15.9g protein; 6.2g fibre

1 large red onion (300g), chopped coarsely
1 chorizo sausage (170g), chopped coarsely
1 large red capsicum (bell pepper) (350g),
chopped coarsely
2 teaspoons smoked paprika
800g (1½ pounds) canned borlotti beans,
rinsed, drained
800g (1½ pounds) canned crushed tomatoes
2 tablespoons coarsely chopped fresh
flat-leaf parsley

1 Heat oiled large saucepan; cook onion,
chorizo and capsicum, stirring, until
vegetables are tender. Add paprika; cook,
stirring, until fragrant.
2 Add beans and undrained tomatoes to pan;
bring to the boil. Reduce heat; simmer,
uncovered, about 5 minutes or until sauce is
thickened.
3 Serve sprinkled with parsley.
tip **Serve with crusty bread.**

BEEF RISSOLES
WITH BEETROOT SALAD

prep + cook time **20 minutes** serves **2**
nutritional count per serving **8.9g total fat**
(3.4g saturated fat); 949kJ (227 cal);
7.9g carbohydrate; 27.1g protein; 2.9g fibre

220g lean minced (ground) beef
1 clove garlic, crushed
2 teaspoons ground cumin
cooking-oil spray
210g (6½ ounces) canned baby beets,
drained, halved
⅓ cup coarsely chopped fresh
flat-leaf parsley
3 green onions (scallions), sliced thinly
1 tablespoon balsamic vinegar
2 tablespoons low-fat cottage cheese

1 Combine beef, garlic and cumin in small
bowl; shape mixture into four patties.
2 Spray medium frying pan with cooking oil;
heat pan. Cook patties in pan.
3 Meanwhile, combine beetroot, parsley, onion
and vinegar in medium bowl.
4 Serve salad topped with patties and
dolloped with cheese.

smoky beans with chorizo

chicken and pumpkin tortilla

CHICKEN AND PUMPKIN TORTILLA

prep + cook time **20 minutes** serves **2**
nutritional count per serving **6.4g total fat
(1.5g saturated fat); 1195kJ (286 cal);
26.1g carbohydrate; 29.1g protein; 3.0g fibre**

**160g (5 ounces) chicken breast fillet
1 tablespoon taco seasoning mix
cooking-oil spray
150g (4½ ounces) butternut pumpkin, cut
    into 1cm (½-inch) cubes
2 tablespoons coarsely chopped fresh
    coriander (cilantro)
⅓ cup (65g) low-fat cottage cheese
2 green onions (scallions), chopped finely
2 tablespoons lime juice
1 clove garlic, crushed
2 x 15cm (6-inch) flour tortillas**

1 Combine chicken and seasoning mix in
small bowl.
2 Spray chicken with cooking oil; cook
chicken, on one side, in heated medium frying
pan 5 minutes. Turn chicken; add pumpkin.
Cook chicken and pumpkin, uncovered,
about 5 minutes or until both are cooked.
3 Chop chicken coarsely; combine in medium
bowl with pumpkin and coriander.
4 Combine cheese, onion, juice and garlic in
small bowl.
5 Spread cheese mixture, then chicken mixture
on one tortilla; top with remaining tortilla. Serve
cut into wedges.

cumin fish with roasted corn salsa

CUMIN FISH WITH ROASTED CORN SALSA

prep + cook time **20 minutes** serves **2**
nutritional count per serving **5.7g total fat
(1.2g saturated fat); 1534kJ (367 cal);
33.6g carbohydrate; 39.9g protein; 9.5g fibre**

**2 trimmed corn cobs (500g)
⅓ cup coarsely chopped fresh
    coriander (cilantro)
1 small red capsicum (bell pepper) (150g),
    chopped finely
3 green onions (scallions), chopped finely
2 tablespoons lime juice
300g (9½ ounces) firm white fish fillets
1 teaspoon ground cumin**

1 Cut kernels from corn cobs; roast corn in
heated medium frying pan, stirring constantly.
Transfer to medium bowl.
2 Stir in coriander, capsicum, onion and juice.
3 Sprinkle fish with cumin; cook in same
heated pan.
4 Serve corn salsa topped with fish. Serve with
lime wedges, if you like.

STIR-FRIED CHOY SUM

prep + cook time **15 minutes** serves **4**
nutritional count per serving **8.9g total fat**
(1.9g saturated fat); 744kJ (178 cal);
1.8g carbohydrate; 21.6g protein; 2.1g fibre

Heat 1 tablespoon peanut oil in wok; stir-fry
1 thinly sliced fresh long red chilli, 2 crushed
cloves garlic and 2cm (¾-inch) piece grated
fresh ginger until fragrant. Add 1kg (2 pounds)
trimmed, coarsely chopped choy sum; stir-fry
until almost tender. Add 2 tablespoons fish
sauce and 2 tablespoons lime juice; stir-fry
until hot. Serve sprinkled with 1 cup roasted
unsalted cashews and lime wedges, if you like.

BRUSSELS SPROUTS WITH CREAM

prep + cook time **10 minutes** serves **4**
nutritional count per serving **46.7g total fat**
(28.4g saturated fat); 2061kJ (493 cal);
6.6g carbohydrate; 9.5g protein; 7.3g fibre

Melt 15g (½ ounce) of butter in large frying
pan; cook ⅓ cup (25g) flaked almonds, stirring,
until browned lightly; remove from pan. Melt
50g (1½ ounces) butter in same pan; cook
1kg (2 pounds) trimmed, halved brussels
sprouts and 2 cloves crushed garlic, stirring,
until sprouts are browned lightly. Add 1¼ cups
(310ml) pouring cream; bring to the boil.
Reduce heat; simmer, uncovered, until sprouts
are tender and sauce thickens slightly. Serve
sprout mixture sprinkled with nuts.
tip **It is fine to just use 1 x 300ml carton of cream for**
this recipe.

SPEEDY SIDES

MIXED CABBAGE COLESLAW

prep time **20 minutes** serves **4**
nutritional count per serving **18.4g total fat**
(2.6g saturated fat); 836kJ (200 cal);
4.5g carbohydrate; 2.4g protein; 4.7g fibre

Whisk ⅓ cup (80ml) olive oil, 2 tablespoons
cider vinegar and 2 teaspoons dijon mustard in
large bowl; mix in 2 cups finely shredded green
cabbage, 2 cups finely shredded red cabbage,
2 cups finely shredded wombok (napa
cabbage), 1 coarsely grated medium carrot
and 4 thinly sliced green onions (scallions).

PEAS WITH MINT BUTTER

prep + cook time **10 minutes** serves **4**
nutritional count per serving **8.6g total fat**
(5.4g saturated fat); 589kJ (141 cal);
8.6g carbohydrate; 5.2g protein; 5g fibre

Boil, steam or microwave 2¼ cups (360g)
fresh shelled peas until tender; drain.
Meanwhile, combine 40g (1½ ounces)
softened butter, 1 tablespoon finely chopped
fresh mint and 1 teaspoon finely grated lemon
rind in small bowl. Serve peas topped with
butter mixture.

SMOKY BARBECUE BEEF STEAKS

prep + cook time 15 minutes serves 4
nutritional count per serving 13.3g total fat
(5.5g saturated fat); 1459kJ (349 cal);
10.1g carbohydrate; 46.7g protein; 0.5g fibre

¼ cup (60ml) barbecue sauce
2 tablespoons tomato sauce (ketchup)
1 teaspoon smoked paprika
2 teaspoons cider vinegar
1 clove garlic, crushed
4 beef sirloin steaks (880g)

1 Combine sauces, paprika, vinegar and garlic
in large bowl with steaks.
2 Cook steaks on heated oiled grill plate (or grill
or barbecue), brushing frequently with marinade.

GRILLS
& BBQS

GRILLED LAMB CHOPS WITH TOMATO AND OLIVE SALSA

prep + cook time **10 minutes** serves **4**
nutritional count per serving **16.2g total fat**
(6.6g saturated fat); 1333kJ (319 cal);
8.2g carbohydrate; 33.9g protein; 2.2g fibre

¼ cup loosely packed fresh oregano leaves
8 lamb loin chops (800g)
250g (8 ounces) cherry tomatoes, quartered
½ cup (75g) seeded kalamata olives, halved
2 tablespoons french dressing
100g (3 ounces) rocket (arugula) leaves

1 Finely chop half the oregano; combine with lamb in large bowl.
2 Season lamb; cook on heated oiled grill pan (or grill or barbecue).
3 Meanwhile, combine tomato, olives, dressing and remaining oregano in medium bowl. Serve chops with salsa and rocket.

sumac chicken with minted eggplant

SUMAC CHICKEN WITH MINTED EGGPLANT

prep + cook time **20 minutes** serves **4**
nutritional count per serving **28.3g total fat**
(5.7g saturated fat); 2107kJ (504 cal);
14.2g carbohydrate; 45.9g protein; 5.1g fibre

1 teaspoon finely grated lemon rind
⅓ cup (80ml) lemon juice
2 teaspoons sumac
2 teaspoons caster (superfine) sugar
1 tablespoon tahini
800g (1½ pounds) chicken tenderloins
2 medium eggplants (600g), sliced thickly
¼ cup (60ml) olive oil
½ cup coarsely chopped fresh mint
1 lemon (140g), sliced thickly

1 Combine rind, half the juice, sumac, sugar, tahini and chicken in large bowl.
2 Cook chicken on heated oiled grill plate (or grill or barbecue) until cooked. Remove from heat; cover to keep warm.
3 Cook eggplant on cleaned heated oiled grill plate until browned; combine eggplant in medium bowl with remaining juice, oil and mint.
4 Serve chicken and eggplant with lemon.

grilled lamb chops with tomato and olive salsa

ORANGE AND SOY SALMON PARCELS

prep + cook time **20 minutes** serves **4**
nutritional count per serving **14.8g total fat**
(3.2g saturated fat); 1471kJ (352 cal);
6.2g carbohydrate; 45.6g protein; 5.6g fibre

4 x 200g (6½-ounce) salmon fillets
4 green onions (scallions), sliced thinly
1cm (½-inch) piece fresh ginger (5g),
   sliced thinly
2 cloves garlic, sliced thinly
¼ cup (60ml) light soy sauce
1 tablespoon finely grated orange rind
⅓ cup (80ml) orange juice
2 teaspoons grated palm sugar
450g (14½ ounces) baby buk choy,
   chopped coarsely
350g (11 ounces) broccolini,
   halved crossways

1 Place each fish fillet on a piece of lightly oiled foil large enough to completely enclose fish. Combine onion, ginger, garlic, sauce, rind, juice and sugar in small jug; divide mixture among fish pieces. Gather corners of foil above fish; twist to enclose securely.

2 Cook parcels on heated oiled grill plate (or grill or barbecue) about 5 minutes or until fish is cooked as desired.

3 Meanwhile, boil, steam or microwave buk choy and broccolini, separately, until tender; drain. Serve salmon with vegetables.

grilled lamb with paprikash sauce

GRILLED LAMB
WITH PAPRIKASH SAUCE

prep + cook time **15 minutes** serves **4**
nutritional count per serving **12g total fat**
(3.8g saturated fat); 1241kJ (297 cal);
4.4g carbohydrate; 42.1g protein; 1.6g fibre

800g (1½ pounds) lamb backstraps
1 tablespoon olive oil
1 small brown onion (80g), chopped finely
1 clove garlic, crushed
1 teaspoon smoked paprika
2 teaspoons sweet paprika
pinch cayenne pepper
410g (13 ounces) canned crushed tomatoes
½ cup (125ml) water

1 Cook lamb on heated oiled grill plate
(or grill or barbecue). Cover; stand 5 minutes
then slice thickly.
2 Meanwhile, heat oil in medium saucepan;
cook onion, stirring, until onion softens. Add
garlic and spices; cook, stirring, about 1 minute
or until fragrant.
3 Add undrained tomatoes and the water;
bring to the boil. Reduce heat; simmer,
uncovered, about 5 minutes or until paprikash
sauce thickens slightly.
4 Serve lamb with sauce.

VEAL CUTLETS WITH PEAR
AND PISTACHIO SALSA

prep + cook time **15 minutes** serves **4**
nutritional count per serving **11.4g total fat**
(1.8g saturated fat); 1078kJ (258 cal);
12.3g carbohydrate; 24.7g protein; 3.5g fibre

4 veal cutlets (500g)
1 small orange (180g)
2 medium pears (460g), unpeeled,
**   chopped finely**
¼ cup (35g) pistachios, roasted,
**   chopped finely**
⅓ cup finely chopped fresh flat-leaf parsley
1 tablespoon olive oil

1 Cook veal on heated oiled grill plate (or grill
or barbecue).
2 Meanwhile, finely grate 1 teaspoon rind from
orange. Squeeze juice from orange (you need
¼ cup (60ml) juice).
3 To make salsa, combine rind and juice in
medium bowl with remaining ingredients. Serve
veal topped with salsa.

veal cutlets with pear and pistachio salsa

satay pork medallions

SATAY PORK MEDALLIONS

prep + cook time **15 minutes** serves **4**
nutritional count per serving **23.9g total fat**
(8.7g saturated fat); 1655kJ (396 cal);
4.6g carbohydrate; 39.7g protein; 2.8g fibre

4 pork loin steaks (600g)
¼ cup (70g) crunchy peanut butter
⅓ cup (80ml) coconut cream
2 tablespoons sweet chilli sauce
2 teaspoons fish sauce
1 tablespoon coarsely chopped fresh
   coriander (cilantro)

1 Cook pork on heated oiled grill plate
(or grill or barbecue).
2 Meanwhile, combine peanut butter,
coconut cream, sauces and ¼ cup (60ml)
water in small saucepan; cook, stirring, over
heat about 3 minutes or until thickened slightly.
3 Serve pork drizzled with sauce; sprinkle
with coriander.

grilled prawns with lemon grass and lime

GRILLED PRAWNS
WITH LEMON GRASS AND LIME

prep + cook time **10 minutes** serves **4**
nutritional count per serving **13.1g total fat**
(8.2g saturated fat); 928kJ (222 cal);
0.3g carbohydrate; 25.9g protein; 0.2g fibre

60g (2 ounces) butter, softened
10cm (4-inch) stick fresh lemon grass (20g),
   chopped finely
2 teaspoons finely grated lime rind
2 tablespoons lime juice
2 tablespoons finely chopped fresh
   flat-leaf parsley
500g (1 pound) shelled uncooked medium
   king prawns (shrimp)

1 Beat butter, lemon grass, rind and juice in
small bowl until combined; stir in parsley.
2 Melt half the butter mixture in large frying
pan; remove from heat, stir in prawns.
3 Cook prawns on heated oiled barbecue
(or grill or grill pan) until changed in colour.
Serve prawns topped with remaining
butter mixture.

grilled chicken, brie and avocado on ciabatta

BEEF SKEWERS WITH GREEK SALAD

prep + cook time **20 minutes** serves **4**
nutritional count per serving **5.4g total fat**
(1.8g saturated fat); 1020kJ (244 cal);
8.7g carbohydrate; 37.8g protein; 4.0g fibre

300g (9½ ounces) beef rump steak, cut
into 2cm (¾-inch) cubes
1 tablespoon finely chopped fresh thyme
cooking-oil spray
2 small tomatoes (190g), chopped coarsely
1 small green capsicum (bell pepper) (150g),
chopped coarsely
¼ cup (30g) seeded black olives
1 lebanese cucumber (130g),
chopped coarsely
¼ cup coarsely chopped fresh
flat-leaf parsley
1 lemon

1 Combine beef and thyme in medium bowl;
thread beef onto skewers. Spray beef with
cooking oil; cook skewers on heated grill plate
(or grill or barbecue).
2 Meanwhile, combine remaining ingredients in
medium bowl.
3 Serve salad with beef skewers and lemon
wedges, if desired.

GRILLED CHICKEN, BRIE AND AVOCADO ON CIABATTA

prep + cook time **20 minutes** serves **4**
nutritional count per serving **22.6g total fat**
(8.3g saturated fat); 1768kJ (423 cal);
22.9g carbohydrate; 30.6g protein; 2.9g fibre

2 chicken breast fillets (400g)
4 thick slices ciabatta bread (140g)
⅓ cup (80ml) sweet chilli sauce
50g (1½ ounces) baby rocket (arugula) leaves
100g (3 ounces) brie cheese, cut into 4 slices
1 small avocado (200g), sliced thinly

1 Halve chicken pieces diagonally; slice
through each piece horizontally (you will have
8 pieces). Cook on heated oiled grill plate
(or grill or barbecue) until chicken is browned
both sides and cooked through.
2 Toast bread, both sides, on same grill plate.
3 Spread half the sauce over toast slices; top
with rocket, chicken, cheese then avocado.
Drizzle with remaining sauce.

beef skewers with greek salad

mexican pork cutlets with avocado salsa

MEXICAN PORK CUTLETS WITH AVOCADO SALSA

prep + cook time **20 minutes** serves **4**
nutritional count per serving **42.2g total fat**
(10.7g saturated fat); 2241kJ (536 cal);
1.2g carbohydrate; 38g protein; 1.2g fibre

2 tablespoons taco seasoning mix
¼ cup (60ml) olive oil
4 x 235g (7½-ounce) pork cutlets
3 small tomatoes (270g), seeded,
    chopped finely
1 small avocado (200g), chopped finely
1 lebanese cucumber (130g), seeded,
    chopped finely
1 tablespoon lime juice

1 Combine seasoning mix, 2 tablespoons of
the oil and pork in large bowl. Cook pork on
heated oiled grill plate (or grill or barbecue)
until cooked.
2 Meanwhile, combine remaining oil in medium
bowl with tomato, avocado, cucumber and
juice. Serve pork with salsa.

chicken yakitori with sesame dipping sauce

CHICKEN YAKITORI WITH SESAME DIPPING SAUCE

prep + cook time **20 minutes** serves **4**
nutritional count per serving **20.4g total fat**
(6.4g saturated fat); 1643kJ (393 cal);
3.8g carbohydrate; 47.1g protein; 0.1g fibre

12 chicken tenderloins (1kg)
sesame dipping sauce
¼ cup (60ml) light soy sauce
2 tablespoons mirin
3 teaspoons white sugar
½ teaspoon sesame oil
1 teaspoon sesame seeds

1 Make sesame dipping sauce.
2 Thread each tenderloin onto a skewer; brush
skewers with half the dipping sauce.
3 Cook skewers, in batches, in heated oiled
grill pan (or grill or barbecue) until chicken is
cooked. Serve skewers with remaining sesame
dipping sauce.
sesame dipping sauce Combine ingredients
in small saucepan; stir over medium heat until
sugar dissolves.

CARAMEL BANANA SPLIT

prep + cook time **15 minutes** serves **4**
nutritional count per serving **32.4g total fat**
(19.5g saturated fat); 2383kJ (570 cal);
60g carbohydrate; 10.1g protein; 2.5g fibre

Whisk ½ cup caramel top'n'fill and ¼ cup (60ml) thickened (heavy) cream in small saucepan over low heat until smooth. Beat ½ cup (125ml) extra thickened (heavy) cream in small bowl with electric mixer until soft peaks form. Peel then cut 4 small bananas in half lengthways; place in serving dishes. Top bananas with scoops of vanilla ice-cream and whipped cream; drizzle with caramel sauce and sprinkle with 2 tablespoons crushed peanuts. Serve banana splits with 8 slices almond bread.

CHOC-CHERRY AND HAZELNUT BISCOTTI TRIFLE

prep time **15 minutes** serves **4**
nutritional count per serving **18.8g total fat**
(10.4g saturated fat); 1935kJ (463 cal);
56.4g carbohydrate; 10.1g protein; 2.4g fibre

Combine 300g (9½ ounces) thawed frozen pitted black cherries and ⅓ cup (80ml) marsala in small bowl. Reserve 8 biscotti from 170g (5½ ounces) chocolate hazelnut biscotti; chop remaining biscotti coarsely. Place 6 x 62g (2-ounce) tubs chocolate mousse in medium bowl; whisk until smooth. Spoon half the cherry mixture into 4 x 2-cup (500ml) serving glasses; top with half the chopped biscotti and half the mousse. Repeat layering. Serve trifles with reserved biscotti.

SPEEDY DESSERTS

CREPES WITH ICE CREAM AND PASSIONFRUIT SAUCE

prep time **10 minutes** serves **4**
nutritional count per serving **31.3g total fat**
(19.3g saturated fat); 1990kJ (476 cal);
36g carbohydrate; 10.6g protein; 5.3g fibre

Warm ¾ cup (180ml) pouring cream in small saucepan over low heat; remove from heat, stir in ½ cup passionfruit pulp. Heat 400g (12½-ounce) packet frozen crêpes according to directions on the packet. Serve crêpes with sauce and scoops of ice-cream.

RASPBERRY COCONUT CREAM

prep time **15 minutes** serves **6**
nutritional count per serving **28.3g total fat**
(18.8g saturated fat); 1526kJ (365 cal);
23.6g carbohydrate; 3.5g protein; 2.6g fibre

Whip 1¼ cups (310ml) thickened (heavy) cream and 2 tablespoons sifted icing (confectioners') sugar in small bowl with electric mixer until soft peaks form; transfer to medium bowl. Fold in ⅔ cup (160ml) thick vanilla custard and 100g (3 ounces) crumbled coconut macaroons. Layer into serving glasses with 125g (4 ounces) fresh or frozen raspberries; top with crumbled chocolate flake.

TERIYAKI SALMON

prep + cook time **10 minutes** serves **4**
nutritional count per serving **15.6g total fat**
(3.5g saturated fat); 1404kJ (336 cal);
3.8g carbohydrate; 43.5g protein; 0.1g fibre

Heat oiled large frying pan; cook 4 salmon
fillets, skin-side down, about 5 minutes or until
skin is crisp. Turn fish; add 2 tablespoons
japanese soy sauce to pan with 2 tablespoons
mirin, 2 tablespoons water and 1 tablespoon
light brown sugar; simmer, uncovered, until
salmon is cooked as desired. Serve salmon
sprinkled with 1 thinly sliced green onion
(scallion). Drizzle over pan juices.

SIMPLE STEAK SANDWICHES

prep + cook time **10 minutes** serves **4**
nutritional count per serving **15.9g total fat**
(4.7g saturated fat); 2646kJ (633 cal);
72.1g carbohydrate; 45.4g protein; 8.4g fibre

Season 4 x 150g (4½-ounce) beef scotch fillet
steaks well on both sides. Cook beef on
heated oiled barbecue (or grill or grill pan).
Spread ¼ cup (75g) dijonnaise on 8 thick slices
toasted ciabatta bread. Sandwich with 50g
(1½ ounces) mixed salad leaves, steaks,
2 thickly sliced medium tomatoes and ⅓ cup
capsicum (bell pepper) relish between
toast slices.

PAPPARDELLE CARBONARA

prep + cook time **10 minutes** serves **4**
nutritional count per serving **22.6g total fat**
(12.7g saturated fat); 2349kJ (562 cal);
65g carbohydrate; 22.7g protein; 3.3g fibre

Cook 375g (12 ounces) pappardelle pasta in
large saucepan of boiling water until just
tender; drain, reserving ½ cup (125ml) cooking
liquid. Return pasta to pan over low heat.
Meanwhile, cook 8 slices thinly sliced
prosciutto in heated oiled large frying pan
until crisp; remove from pan. Combine 3 eggs,
½ cup (125ml) pouring cream and ½ cup (40g)
finely grated parmesan cheese in large jug.
Add egg mixture, reserved pasta water,
1½ tablespoons finely chopped fresh flat-leaf
parsley and half the prosciutto to pasta;
toss gently. Serve pasta topped with 1½
tablespoons finely chopped fresh flat-leaf
parsley and remaining prosciutto; season
with pepper.

CHEESY HAM OMELETTE

prep + cook time **10 minutes** serves **4**
nutritional count per serving **25.8g total fat**
(12.8g saturated fat); 1425kJ (341 cal);
0.5g carbohydrate; 27.3g protein; 0.1g fibre

Combine 125g (4 ounces) finely chopped
smoked ham and ⅔ cup (80g) coarsely grated
gruyère cheese in a small bowl. Beat 8 egg
whites in large bowl with electric mixer until
soft peaks form. Combine 8 egg yolks,
1½ tablespoons finely chopped fresh chives
and ⅓ cup (25g) finely grated parmesan
cheese in large bowl. Gently fold egg whites
into yolk mixture. Heat 10g (½ ounce) butter in
a small frying pan; add one-quarter of the egg
mixture, sprinkle with one-quarter of the ham
mixture. Cook over medium heat until mixture
is almost set. Fold omelette in half, transfer to
plate; sprinkle with 1 teaspoon finely chopped
fresh chives. Cover to keep warm. Repeat to
make a further 3 omelettes.

MEALS IN 10 MINUTES

HONEY MUSTARD LAMB CUTLETS

prep + cook time **10 minutes** serves **4**
nutritional count per serving **13.2g total fat**
(5.9g saturated fat); 1058kJ (253 cal);
4.5g carbohydrate; 17.7g protein; 2.9g fibre

Combine 1 tablespoon each dijon and
wholegrain mustards, 2 tablespoons honey
and 1 tablespoon white wine vinegar in small
jug. Combine half the honey mixture in large
bowl; with 12 french-trimmed lamb cutlets.
Cook lamb in heated oiled large frying pan.
Meanwhile, boil, steam or microwave 400g
(12½ ounces) trimmed green beans until
tender; drain. Serve lamb with green beans;
drizzle with remaining honey mixture.

MOROCCAN CHICKEN

prep + cook time **10 minutes** serves **4**
nutritional count per serving **13g total fat**
(2.6g saturated fat); 2600kJ (622 cal);
60.4g carbohydrate; 63.3g protein; 2.5g fibre

Sprinkle 12 chicken tenderloins with
2 tablespoons moroccan seasoning; cook
in heated oiled large frying pan. Meanwhile,
combine 1¼ cups (250g) couscous, 1¼ cups
(310ml) boiling water in large heatproof bowl,
cover; stand about 5 minutes or until water is
absorbed, fluffing with fork occasionally. Stir in
⅓ cup (55g) sultanas, ⅓ cup (45g) roasted
slivered almonds and ½ cup coarsely chopped
fresh coriander (cilantro). Divide couscous
among serving bowls; top with chicken and
½ cup (140g) yogurt.

GARLIC CHILLI MUSSELS

prep + cook time **10 minutes** serves **4**
nutritional count per serving **13.3g total fat**
(8.4g saturated fat); 702kJ (168 cal);
2.8g carbohydrate; 6.3g protein; 0.6g fibre

Heat 60g (2 ounces) chopped butter, 3 cloves
crushed garlic and 1 thinly sliced fresh long red
chilli in large saucepan, stirring, until fragrant.
Add ⅓ cup (80ml) dry white wine; bring to the
boil. Add 1kg (2 pounds) cleaned small black
mussels to pan; simmer, covered, until mussels
open (discard any that do not). Stir in ⅓ cup
coarsely chopped fresh flat-leaf parsley.

TOMATO AND PROSCIUTTO SALAD

prep + cook time **10 minutes** serves **4**
nutritional count per serving **31.2g total fat**
(11.2g saturated fat); 1488kJ (356 cal);
1.8g carbohydrate; 16.9g protein; 2.1g fibre

Cook 3 slices prosciutto in heated medium
frying pan until crisp; drain on absorbent paper.
When cool enough to handle, break into
pieces. Combine prosciutto, 3 coarsely
chopped large egg (plum) tomatoes,
300g (9½ ounces) coarsely chopped cherry
bocconcini cheese, 1 coarsely chopped
medium avocado and 125g (4 ounces) mixed
salad leaves in serving bowl. Drizzle with
2 tablespoons olive oil.

ALMONDS flat, pointy-tipped nuts with a pitted brown shell enclosing a creamy white kernel which is covered by a brown skin.

blanched brown skins removed.

flaked paper-thin slices.

meal also known as ground almonds.

slivered small pieces cut lengthways.

BEAN SPROUTS also called bean shoots; tender new growths of beans and seeds germinated for consumption as sprouts.

BEETROOT also known as red beets; firm, round root vegetable.

BROCCOLINI a cross between broccoli and chinese kale; long asparagus-like stems with a long loose floret, both completely edible. Resembles broccoli but is milder and sweeter in taste.

BUK CHOY also known as bok choy, pak choi, chinese white cabbage or chinese chard; has a fresh, mild mustard taste. Use stems and leaves, stir-fried or braised. Baby buk choy is much smaller and more tender. Its mildly acrid, distinctively appealing taste has made it one of the most commonly used asian greens.

CABANOSSI a ready-to-eat sausage; also known as cabana.

CAPERS the grey-green buds of a warm climate (usually Mediterranean) shrub, sold either dried and salted or pickled in a vinegar brine; tiny young ones, called baby capers, are also available in brine or dried in salt.

CAPSICUM also called pepper or bell pepper. Discard seeds and membranes before use.

CHICKPEAS also called garbanzos, hummus or channa; an irregularly round, sandy-coloured legume used extensively in Mediterranean, Indian and Hispanic cooking. Firm texture even after cooking, a floury mouth-feel and robust nutty flavour; available canned or dried (reconstitute for several hours in cold water before use).

CHINESE COOKING WINE also called shao hsing or chinese rice wine; made from fermented rice, wheat, sugar and salt with a 13.5 per cent alcohol content. Inexpensive and found in Asian food shops; if you can't find it, replace with mirin or sherry.

CHORIZO a sausage of Spanish origin, made of coarsely ground pork and highly seasoned with garlic and chilli.

CHOY SUM also known as pakaukeo or flowering cabbage, a member of the buk choy family; easy to identify with its long stems, light green leaves and yellow flowers. Stems and leaves are both edible, steamed or stir-fried.

CORIANDER also called cilantro, pak chee or chinese parsley; bright-green-leafed herb with both pungent aroma and taste. Coriander seeds are dried and sold either whole or ground, and neither form tastes remotely like the fresh leaf.

COUSCOUS a fine, grain-like cereal product made from semolina; from North Africa. A semolina flour and water dough is sieved then dehydrated to produce minuscule even-sized pellets of couscous; it is rehydrated by steaming or with the addition of a warm liquid and swells to three or four times its original size; eaten like rice with a tagine.

CRAISINS dried cranberries.

CREAM we used fresh cream, also known as pure or pouring cream unless otherwise stated. Has no additives. Minimum fat content 35 per cent.

sour a thick, commercially cultured sour cream with a minimum fat content of 35 per cent; light sour cream has 18.5 per cent fat.

thick (double) a dolloping cream with a minimum fat content of 45 per cent.

thickened (heavy) a whipping cream containing thickener. Minimum fat content 35 per cent.

CUMIN also known as zeera or comino; resembling caraway in size, cumin is the seed of a plant related to the parsley family with a spicy, almost curry-like flavour is essential to the traditional foods. Available dried as seeds or ground.

ENDIVE, CURLY also known as frisée, a curly-leafed green vegetable, mainly used in salads.

FISH SAUCE called naam pla on the label if Thai-made, nuoc naam if Vietnamese; the two are almost identical. Made from pulverised salted fermented fish (most often anchovies); has a pungent smell and strong taste.

FIVE-SPICE POWDER although the ingredients vary from country to country, five-spice is usually a fragrant mixture of ground cinnamon, cloves, star anise, sichuan pepper and fennel seeds.

GAI LAN also known as gai larn, chinese broccoli and chinese kale; green vegetable appreciated more for its stems than its coarse leaves. Can be served steamed and stir-fried, in soups and noodle dishes.

GLOSSARY

GREEN ONION also known as scallion or (incorrectly) shallot; an immature onion picked before the bulb has formed, having a long, bright-green edible stalk.

HARISSA a north african paste made from dried red chillies, garlic, olive oil and caraway seeds; can be used as a rub for meat, an ingredient in sauces and dressings, or eaten as a condiment. It is available from Middle Eastern food shops and some supermarkets.

HOISIN SAUCE a thick, sweet and spicy chinese barbecue sauce made from salted fermented soybeans, onions and garlic; used as a marinade or baste, or to accent stir-fries and barbecued or roasted foods. From Asian food shops and supermarkets.

KAFFIR LIME LEAVES also known as bai magrood and looks like two glossy dark green leaves joined end to end, forming a rounded hourglass shape. Used fresh or dried in many South-East Asian dishes; a strip of fresh lime peel may be substituted for each leaf.

LEMON GRASS also known as takrai, serai or serah. A tall, clumping, lemon-smelling and tasting, sharp-edged aromatic tropical grass; the white lower part of the stem is used, finely chopped, in the cooking of South-East Asia.

LETTUCE

butter also known as a boston lettuce, has small, round, loosely formed heads with a sweet flavour; soft, buttery-textured leaves range from pale green on the outer leaves to pale yellow-green inner leaves.

cos also known as romaine lettuce; the traditional caesar salad lettuce. Long, with leaves ranging from dark green on the outside to almost white near the core; the leaves have a stiff centre rib giving a slight cupping effect to the leaf on either side.

mesclun pronounced mess-kluhn; also known as mixed greens or spring salad mix. A commercial blend of assorted young lettuce and other green leaves.

radicchio Italian in origin; a member of the chicory family. The dark burgundy leaves and strong, bitter flavour can be cooked or eaten raw in salads.

MILK we use full-cream homogenised milk unless otherwise specified.

buttermilk in spite of its name, buttermilk is actually low in fat, varying between 0.6 per cent and 2.0 per cent per 100ml. Originally the term given to the slightly sour liquid left after butter was churned from cream, today it is intentionally made from no-fat or low-fat milk to which specific bacterial cultures have been added during the manufacturing process.

MIRIN a japanese champagne-coloured cooking wine, made of glutinous rice and alcohol. It is used expressly for cooking and should not be confused with sake.

MUSTARD

dijon also called french. Pale brown, creamy, distinctively flavoured, fairly mild french mustard.

wholegrain also known as seeded. A french-style coarse-grain mustard made from crushed mustard seeds and dijon-style french mustard. Works well with cold meats and sausages.

NOODLES

dried rice noodles also known as rice stick noodles. Made from rice flour and water, available flat and wide or very thin (vermicelli). Must be soaked in boiling water to soften.

fresh egg also called ba mee or yellow noodles; made from wheat flour and eggs, sold fresh or dried. Range in size from very fine strands to wide, spaghetti-like pieces as thick as a shoelace.

fresh rice also called ho fun, khao pun, sen yau, pho or kway tiau, depending on the country of manufacture; the most common form of noodle used in Thailand. Can be purchased in strands of various widths or large sheets weighing about 500g which are to be cut into the desired noodle size. Chewy and pure white, they do not need pre-cooking before use.

rice vermicelli also known as sen mee, mei fun or bee hoon. Used throughout Asia in spring rolls and cold salads; similar to bean threads, only longer and made with rice flour instead of mung bean starch. Before using, soak the dried noodles in hot water until softened, boil them briefly then rinse with hot water. Vermicelli can also be deep-fried until crunchy and used in salad or as a garnish or bed for sauces.

soba thin, pale-brown noodle originally from Japan; made from buckwheat and varying proportions of wheat flour. Available dried and fresh; eaten in soups, stir-fries and, chilled, on their own.

udon available fresh and dried, these broad, white, wheat japanese noodles.

PAPRIKA ground dried sweet red capsicum (bell pepper); there are many grades and types, including sweet, hot, mild and smoked.

PIRI PIRI SAUCE a portuguese chilli sauce made from red chillies, ginger, garlic, oil and various herbs.

POMEGRANATE dark-red, leathery-skinned fresh fruit about the size of an orange filled with hundreds of seeds, each wrapped in an edible crimson pulp with a unique tangy sweet-sour flavour.

RICE PAPER ROUNDS also known as banh trang, made from rice paste and stamped into rounds; store well at room temperature. They're quite brittle and will break if dropped; dipped momentarily in water they become pliable wrappers for fried food and uncooked vegetables.

ROCKET also called arugula, rugula and rucola; peppery green leaf eaten raw in salads or used in cooking. Baby rocket leaves are smaller and less peppery.

SAMBAL OELEK also ulek or olek; an indonesian salty paste made from ground chillies and vinegar.

SILVER BEET also known as swiss chard and incorrectly, spinach; has fleshy stalks and large leaves.

SNOW PEAS also called mangetout; a variety of garden pea, eaten pod and all (although you may need to string them). Used in stir-fries or eaten raw in salads. Snow pea sprouts are available from supermarkets or greengrocers and are usually eaten raw in salads or sandwiches.

SOY SAUCE also known as sieu; made from fermented soybeans.

dark deep brown, almost black in colour; rich, with a thicker consistency than other types. Pungent but not particularly salty; good for marinating.

japanese an all-purpose low-sodium soy sauce made with more wheat content than its Chinese counterparts; fermented in barrels and aged. Possibly the best table soy and the one to choose if you only want one variety.

keçap manis a dark, thick sweet soy sauce used in most South-East Asian cuisines. Depending on the manufacturer, the sauces's sweetness is derived from the addition of either molasses or palm sugar when brewed.

STAR ANISE a dried star-shaped pod whose seeds have an astringent aniseed flavour; commonly used to flavour stocks and marinades.

SUGAR we use coarse, granulated table sugar, also known as crystal sugar, unless otherwise specified.

caster also known as superfine or finely granulated table sugar.

palm also called nam tan pip, jaggery, jawa or gula melaka; made from the sap of the sugar palm tree. Light brown to black in colour; you can use brown sugar if palm sugar is unavailable.

SUGAR SNAP PEAS also called honey snap peas; fresh small pea that can be eaten pod and all.

SUMAC a purple-red, astringent spice ground from berries growing on shrubs that flourish wild around the Mediterranean; adds a tart, lemony flavour to dips and dressings and goes well with barbecued meat.

TACO SEASONING MIX a packaged seasoning meant to duplicate the Mexican sauce made from oregano, cumin, chillies and other spices.

TAHINI sesame seed paste available from Middle Eastern food stores.

TAMARI similar to but thicker than japanese soy; very dark in colour with a mellow flavour. Good used as a dipping sauce or for basting.

TORTILLA thin, round unleavened bread originating in Mexico; can be made at home or purchased frozen, fresh or vacuum-packed. Two kinds are available, one made from wheat flour and one from corn.

WITLOF also known as belgian endive; related to and confused with chicory. A versatile vegetable, it tastes as good cooked as it does eaten raw. Grown in darkness like white asparagus to prevent it becoming green; looks somewhat like a tightly furled, cream to very light-green cigar. The leaves can be removed and used to hold a canapé filling; the whole vegetable can be opened up, stuffed then baked or casseroled; and the leaves can be tossed in a salad.

WOMBOK also known as chinese cabbage, peking or napa cabbage; elongated in shape with pale green, crinkly leaves, this is the most common cabbage in South-East Asia. Can be eaten raw or braised, steamed or stir-fried.

ZUCCHINI also known as courgette; belongs to the squash family. Yellow flowers can be stuffed or used in salads.

CONVERSION CHART

MEASURES

One Australian metric measuring cup holds approximately 250ml, one Australian metric tablespoon holds 20ml, one Australian metric teaspoon holds 5ml.

The difference between one country's measuring cups and another's is within a 2- or 3-teaspoon variance, and will not affect your cooking results. North America, New Zealand and the United Kingdom use a 15ml tablespoon. All cup and spoon measurements are level. The most accurate way of measuring dry ingredients is to weigh them. When measuring liquids, use a clear glass or plastic jug with metric markings.

We use large eggs with an average weight of 60g.

DRY MEASURES

METRIC	IMPERIAL
15g	½oz
30g	1oz
60g	2oz
90g	3oz
125g	4oz (¼lb)
155g	5oz
185g	6oz
220g	7oz
250g	8oz (½lb)
280g	9oz
315g	10oz
345g	11oz
375g	12oz (¾lb)
410g	13oz
440g	14oz
470g	15oz
500g	16oz (1lb)
750g	24oz (1½lb)
1kg	32oz (2lb)

LIQUID MEASURES

METRIC	IMPERIAL
30ml	1 fluid oz
60ml	2 fluid oz
100ml	3 fluid oz
125ml	4 fluid oz
150ml	5 fluid oz
190ml	6 fluid oz
250ml	8 fluid oz
300ml	10 fluid oz
500ml	16 fluid oz
600ml	20 fluid oz
1000ml (1 litre)	1¾ pints

LENGTH MEASURES

METRIC	IMPERIAL
3mm	⅛in
6mm	¼in
1cm	½in
2cm	¾in
2.5cm	1in
5cm	2in
6cm	2½in
8cm	3in
10cm	4in
13cm	5in
15cm	6in
18cm	7in
20cm	8in
22cm	9in
25cm	10in
28cm	11in
30cm	12in (1ft)

OVEN TEMPERATURES

These oven temperatures are only a guide for conventional ovens.
For fan-forced ovens, check the manufacturer's manual.

	°C (CELSIUS)	°F (FAHRENHEIT)
Very slow	120	250
Slow	150	275-300
Moderately slow	160	325
Moderate	180	350-375
Moderately hot	200	400
Hot	220	425-450
Very hot	240	475

The imperial measurements used in these recipes are approximate only and should not affect the outcome of your cooking.

If you like this cookbook, you'll love these...

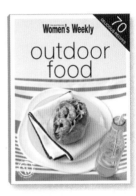

These are just a small selection of titles available in *The Australian Women's Weekly* range
on sale at selected newsagents and supermarkets or online at **www.acpbooks.com.au**